Crossing the Snow Bridge

Crossing the Snow Bridge

Winner of the 1995
Ohio State University Press / *The Journal*
Award in Poetry

Fatima Lim-Wilson

Ohio State University Press
Columbus

Library of Congress Cataloging-in-Publication Data

Lim-Wilson, Fatima, 1961–
    Crossing the snow bridge / Fatima Lim-Wilson.
        p. cm.
    "Winner of the 1995 Ohio State University Press / The journal award
in poetry."
        ISBN 0-8142-0680-8 (cloth : alk. paper). — ISBN 0-8142-0681-6
(paper : alk. paper)
        1. Filipino Americans—Poetry. 2. Philippines—Poetry.
    I. Title.
    PS3562.I4595C76 1995
811'. 54—dc20   95-17599
                                                                CIP

Type set in Monotype Centaur.
Printed by Braun-Brumfield, Inc., Ann Arbor, MI.

9 8 7 6 5 4 3 2 1

Acknowledgments

Some of the poems in this collection have been previously published in the following literary journals:

Alligator Juniper: "Bride of Okura" and "Playing Mahjong with My Father's Ghost"
Asian American Pacific Journal: "Lost Ring" and "A Rice Grain Village"
Crosscurrents: "Alphabet Soup" and "Paper Year"
Dominion Review: "From the Letters to Old Wives"
Field: "Broken English," "Cape Hatteras," and "The Wave"
Forbidden Fruit: Women Writing Erotica: "The Love of Saints"
The Kenyon Review: "Inventing the Filipino" (also reprinted in *The Pushcart Prize XIX: 1994–1995 Best of the Small Presses*)
Manoa: "Luzviminda"
The Massachusetts Review: "From the Bridal Book I"
Poetry: "Primigravida," "Raising the Dead," and "Upon Overhearing Tagalog"
Prairie Schooner: "The Beginning of Things" and "Ringmaster's Wife"
Puerto del Sol: "Pavarotti in Manila"
The Santa Barbara Review: "Amok," "Crossing Dreams," "Things to Do in the Dark"
The Sycamore Review: "Anniversary"
Tamaqua: "Dreaming Magellan" and "Walking with the Dead"

I would also like to thank the Cottages at Hedgebrook, the Seattle Arts Commission, and the King County Arts Commission for their support.

This book is dedicated to

Adrian and Francis Lorenzo Wilson
and Remedios Vengco Lim

Contents

Alphabet Soup, or Mimicry as a Second Language / 3
Upon Overhearing Tagalog / 4
Market Day / 5
Raising the Dead / 6
Pavarotti in Manila / 8
Inventing the Filipino / 10
Positively No Filipinos Allowed / 12
From the Bridal Book I / 14
Amok / 16
Ringmaster's Wife / 18
The Beginning of Things / 19
Primigravida / 21
Pica / 23
From the Letters to Old Wives / 25
Playing Mahjong with My Father's Ghost / 27
Sisters / 29
The Wave / 31
Cape Hatteras / 32
Summer Cottage, Whidbey Island / 33
Anniversary / 35
Bride of Okura / 36
Rice and Fish Sonnet / 39
Dreaming Magellan / 40
My Life in the News / 41
The Man Who Cleaned Her Shoes / 43
Broken English / 45
A Sestina Written in a Cold Land, or There Is No Word for Snow in
    My Language / 47
Luzviminda, or Filipinas Make Such Good Maids / 49
The Resident Alien as Acrobat / 51
A Barren Woman Puts on Her Man Costume / 53

The Weeping Fig / 55
Lost Ring / 56
Our Island / 58
The Dangers of This Craft / 60
Things to Do in the Dark / 62
When They Left Subic Bay / 64
Intuition / 65
Gift of Calamities / 67
Intensity Six: A Call to Dance / 68
The Arsonists / 69
Empty Room / 70
China Patterns / 71
Paper Year / 73
Aubade in Absence / 74
Shot Through / 75
Crossing Dreams / 77
Good Neighbors / 79
Leaving Doors Unlocked / 80
Feeling Amazonian / 81
The Gift Bearer / 82
Farmer Finds Bodies of Student Volunteers / 85
Infant Snatched from Stroller at the Mall / 86
The Love of Saints / 87
From the Bridal Book III / 88
Family Tree / 90
Walking with the Dead / 92
Explaining the Origin of My Name / 93
Kitchen Fires / 96
Forsaken Art / 98
A Rice Grain Village / 99
Translations of Love / 101
From the Bridal Book II / 102
Echo Lake / 103
Ferry to Bainbridge Island / 104
Upon Losing One's Map / 105

Crossing the Snow Bridge

Alphabet Soup, or Mimicry as a Second Language

Angel of letters, feed me.
Beat your wings till I remember
Cardboard cutouts of ABCs. Why
Does my memory hobble, lift
Empty pails from an English castle's dark well?
Fill me with a welter of vowels,
Googol of consonants, tender French
Hearts, dead Latin roots from where words grow,
Insidiously. My tongue smokes, a
Joss stick trailing mixed signals. What
Keeps me from balancing a silver spoon
Locked in my mouth? An echo.
Mother humming her made-up melodies. She
Nudges me to move my lips with hers.
Old wives rustle, whisper tales in my ears.
Palimpsest of longtailed syllables,
Quick darting wings of a windseeking accent.
Run, I must rend the tent of Thesaurus,
Slash away till I warble, silvery voiced with a cut
Tongue. I grow, a hunchback, trailing my master,
Unctuous and anxious. Sweet, mute angel, cast your
Veil over me to muffle the voice of broken glass.
With your flaming sword, mark me, with a bloody
X, to form my lips into singing, always, a heartfelt
Yes. Spewing baubles, I become the favored one. In this
Zoo of sycophants, I'm the parrot who's almost human.

Upon Overhearing Tagalog

Isn't it sweet to hear one's language lift
From the ordered streets? The sparrow
Chatter flies you home, home
To the lullaby din of traffic, the call
Of ripe scents rising from the open markets,
And the sweat's seduction, flesh upon flesh.
Stock-still, you take on that "lost-but-
About-to-be-found" look, sniffing the air,
Tracking down the much missed flock.
Should you rush to them, garlands
Of tears in your eyes, bubbling gratitude
For the singsong signals, the happy
Discord of trivialities overlapping intimacies?
No, you know only too well the scorching
Glare when instant recognition segues
Swiftly into oblivion. Do not dare pass
The parameters of privacy so carefully
Staked out in this territory of strangers.
What you share commands severance.
Avoid the lock of a familiar glance.
Look down, look past, look through,
Masks mouthing a monotone:
Panicked birds retreating, disappearing
Into the manicured orchards of English.

Market Day

Two Filipina maids were forced by their American employer to
march naked down the main street of the Island of Palau.
—*Philippine News*, November 1994

*H*oofbeats thunder roll: dark clouds of runaway horses.
Waterstarved, once-slow-moving buffalo stampede.
We leap higher, higher, insect-winged, monkey brisk,
Forest floor felines, surviving on instinct, dodging
The Spanish master's studded whip, the whistling
Japanese bayonet, the American's made-to-order-
For-us .45. We dance on and on to the music
In our minds, following the path of bats and volcanic
Ash, smiling all the while, drinking our own blood.

The men shadowy under the awnings look, look away,
Look. Even the cut fruit gape and darken. Women
Shiver, feeling the sheerness of their bright blouses.
But no one comes to blanket us, too afraid of our
Moving mirrors, the way we catch and throw back
The sun. And so we dance on, dance till we birth
Tremors under our feet, sending faults racing
Under his very house where the pots we washed
Crash, the child we rocked floats out of its crib.
He alone watches, transfixed, unable to blink,
As we dance, dance on, till we leap out of our skins,
Blinding him with our souls' white flaming.

Raising the Dead

At least 120 people died when a floating shrine sank in the
Bocaue River. Police officer Sonny Pablo said those aboard the
boat were singing and praying.

—*Philippine News*, July 1993

Wreath-heavy, a child's body
Glistens in the sun, cruciform
Among many whose limbs swell
With significance: Last
Breath arrested in grace,
Still singing of Mary's
Embrace of the broken sacrifice
That was her son. His cross
Sprouted from these waters.
This they believe as firmly
As they grip its ragged bark
Swaying upon the shrine.
One touch and tumors melt away,
Lost fortunes turn up in rice pots,
And wandering husbands, remembering
Home, break into a run.
Just as the bleeding woman
In that jostling crowd seared
Christ's hem with the fervor
Of her passing fingers,
Their faith lightnings through
The sacred wood. His love,
Too much to bear, knocks them
Down, down into depths of joy,

The blue robes of an upturned sky.
Their ears ring with their own
Exultance. Their bodies drag new wings.

Pavarotti in Manila

> So the world will know that we are not all kidnappers and maids.
> —Rosemarie "Baby" Arenas, concert organizer

They have built a palace for me
Made of coconuts from ceiling to floor,
Windows facing the sea, and the door
Carved out of old-growth mahogany.
Through the limousine's tinted panes
I wave my signature handkerchief.
As we lumber through the rain,
Beggars cup hands full of grief.
How charming! And not at all alarming.
But my hosts, fashionably pale and piqued,
Dismiss with a flick of haloed wrists
The swarming masses, the red-hot crisis.
Dizziness under the emptyheaded sun.
I rest in my home of dried fronds.
Soundless sweep of servants' feet.
Bulletproof glass deadens the gulls' screech.
Such thoughtfulness, flying in
My favorite wines and choice cheese.
How to practice my trills after such heavy
Meals? Outside, the sea churns
With fishbones and grease. Tomorrow, then
Will I, through the soaked air, hurl
My God's gift of a voice. The noiseless
Sea throws itself against smoky windows.
Tonight, I thrash in the snares of a dream.

Some other music crashes through. Requiem
Of screams. Restless, I flounder
In my tree-thickened nest. Remembering
Yet not recalling this tune. Smirk
Of a too-wise-for-its-own-good moon.
Somewhere, something more frail
Than glass is breaking.

Inventing the Filipino

Let's celebrate the yo-yo makers.
Before you named it "Walking the Dog"
And "Cat's Cradle," our folks
Climbed trees, those agile monkeys,
Knocking down the day's meal
With the world's first yo-yo
Created from twine, a skull-
Sized stone and the spittle
Of gods. What about that jeep
That bounced on the moon? We
Thought of that, too. From
The war's heap you left behind.
When you first landed there
In '69, bouncing like the kids
You are, tossing lunar balls,
Our Miss Philippines pinned on,
Demurely, Miss Universe's crown.
She now rides horses, up and down,
Her makeup artist strategically
Throwing buckets of water
Between her breasts. We have more
Elvises than we can count. And, of
Course, our very own Marie Antoinette,
Who has only you to thank
For the swan-shape of her ankles.
We're a graceful lot, you know.
Great dancers in G-strings,
Especially under the dim of red
Lights. We'd like to join you

Someday, very much. And so
We sway to our sad-sweet songs,
Longing to be the 51st appendix.
Till then we'll fly your flag
Half-mast, over all the hot air
From that blasted god
Thrashing his chains, underground.

Positively No Filipinos Allowed

sign posted outside a hotel, Stockton, California, circa 1930

It was the blind man who carved our front door.
It groaned, heavy with the tumble of fruit
And bleeding fountains. In between the serpent's
Spiral of branches, father and mother
Floated, eyes heavily lidded
And heavenward, their hands petal-folded,
Pious as plump saints. We, nine children,
Knelt below them, openmouthed
With that fixed look of dumb wonder.

I remember how those tepid, trembling fingers
Seemed to steal the very shape of my face.
I made a vow, young as I was, never
To be taken by surprise. Longer
And longer, I stayed away, waiting
For darkness to hide my features
With the death mask of shadows.

Sugared water for the beggars,
Snail-shaped chocolates for the visiting
Archbishop: all were welcome but I
Who wanted to knock down the door
With my own bloodied knuckles.
Father soon spoke of his eight offspring.
Mother's tears and her spent candle wax
Rubbed me out of my hardened heritage.

And now it is America that chisels
Itself into my memory, but I will not
Blink at the glistening monuments,
Nor step back at the approach of oversized
Cars. My hands grow coats of armor
From their bouts with the cold, thorned
Fruit, the repetitive rubbing of my last
Coins. Here, doors are made of glass,
Spinning like windblown pages,
The lobbies within grinning
Like madmen with no teeth and no
Clothes. Nothing still surprises me.

I keep warm with the crisscross
Of my own arms. Memories grow
Stale as bread, but the open air
Does me good. I welcome the rain
With its woman's fingers. My face,
Which in broad daylight is a frightening mask,
Vanishes. Undisturbed, I dream
Of harvesting another barnful
Of fruit, choosing the most
Overripe to throw, like
Grenades, at all closed doors.

*B*efore my groom could pour the gold coins
Upon my open palms, they raised
A sudden cry. Crash of ivory fans,
Missalettes, fainting women knocking
Against the pews. My relatives have found
Us, recognizing me through a smoky veil
In this other country. They walked all the way
In their finery, dropping our gifts
In bushes for rabbits to find. A hammock,
A many-legged crib, and brass fittings
For two coffins. They sang themselves
To exhaustion, carrying Our Lady
Of Sorrows, whose sweat they gathered
In the handkerchief I must put under
My pillow tonight.
An aunt held back the family curse
That locks doors from the inside,
Turns husbands into wolves, grows crosses
On the newborn's back. They gift me
Instead with forgiveness. Why did I hide
Among these naked trees? Winter makes
Their senses keen. They followed
The scent of soursop and three days'
Rain pouring from my skin.
They leave before the first kiss,
Ignoring the groom, gesturing wildly
As if to split open the rawness
Of my belly. They walk more slowly now,

Waiting to hear through falling snow
My soft cries, the ripening pulse
Of their child.

Amok

Amok: In Indonesia and the Philippines, a condition of great
emotional disturbance under which a person loses control and
goes about killing indiscriminately.

—*Webster's New World Dictionary*

*H*e weaves his wife's limbs
With those of her startled lover's.
His sight grows dim as the flowered
Sheets darken. His ears pound with heart's
Hooves, the hoots and footstomping
Of drinking mates who swear
They would do the same and worse.
The fat chickens fall. His child
Cocooning in his hammock and his mother
Calling out the saints and his own holy name
Slow motion into disarray, heaped toys. So, too,
The grinning neighbor and his fenceposts.
Amazingly, the knife gets lighter,
His limbs take on the grace of wings.
Blood petals into patterns, mapping
His rage up and down the street,
The hacking following the beat
Of her sandals sliding
Against the bamboo floor.
She tiptoes to hold onto him, humming,
Her waistlength hair swishing,
Awash in paper lantern light, caked blood.
He whispered the rhythm then:
"One, two, three, keep time with me,

Mahal." Just as he counts
Under his breath now, chasing after
The fading music, erratic, waltzing
With his fleeing shadow, still
Insisting, as he embraces, carves
The air, that he is in full control.

Ringmaster's Wife

You jerk me,
A circus animal in chains,
And my mind suspends tightropes.
I perform on automatic pilot
Doing cartwheels, doing house
Chores, twirling balanced meals
On broom handles, pulling laundry,
Pressed and ironed, out of my sleeves
With the bravura of the hard-
Muscled ballerina. Under the hot
Glare of your wordless commands,
My senses reel, blindly tracking down
The sweetness of the invisible carrot.

Sometimes, you take me out for walks.
I blink in the sun, stiff
In my comical hats and striped suits.
Your friends approve. They throw
Crumbs, loose change. Offer silence
Of the one hand's applause. They praise
You for the diamonds in my eyes.

At night, my dreams pace. Fly over
The big top. I no longer plan escapes.
As you drunkenly throw daggers, never
Missing the heart, I crawl out
Of reach, finding a warm spot
In the darkness of your silken hat,
Between the crooning doves.

The Beginning of Things

Tonight, we make up our own legends.
As we go along, we discover
Buried treasure. Why, when
Touched, does skin raise rows
Of budding flowers, a castle,
Lightning shows? Did you hear
Of the two lovers too entwined
They made the gods so jealous
They had to spend their entire lives
Aching for each other, one turned
Into a rock, the other a bay?
Only, for a few minutes each day
With the tide could they, with rage
And mad laughter, embrace. And so,
I recall their tragedy in the midst
Of our pleasure, taking even more
Time to name and rename the sudden
Dip between the waist and hip,
The regions where lips rest most
At home. I conjure up a full
Moon, chant a forbidden word
Three times, and stir in our
Bed, a pool in whose clear water
I see our future. Kingdom
Of locked limbs, shared breath.
The answers now come flying
Like a winged horse or gold coins
Spilling from a magic purse.
Barefoot, I dance through fire.

I tower over trees. And I bring
To you, still smoking and warm,
The beggar hands of a goddess.

Primigravida

*T*hey stream, invited,
Through the open door
Of my sleeplessness,
The babies born each second,
All saintly, wholly formed.
I have weaved in my mind
Each of their names, their one-
Of-a-kind bibs and sweaters.

I imagine myself an Elizabeth
Waiting by the window
For the vision of Mary
Walking heavily up the steps.
We will look at each other,
Calm with joy, as our children
Shake the crib bars of our bones.

Sometimes I knock myself over
In trying to feel faint,
Forcing life out of my cheeks,
Turning against the very
Scent of fruit. My thoughts,
Growing more potent, can dam,
For a while, the unwelcome
Bloodflow's whirlpooling.
But mind loses over matter.
And my body celebrates, rattling
Its empty cage.

Perhaps tonight, my love
And I can try again.
We shall throw away the charts,
All the well-intentioned charms.
Why wait for a shower of stars?
Perhaps the clocks will grow
Still. An old key
Randomly fished from a pocket
Laughs its way through
Our mothers' doors.
And our bed's iron feet reach
Down, growing roots. Beneath
Us, the dead spin the future
Shape of flowers. If we hold on
To each other, tightly, tightly,
We shall turn over the rocks
Causing the insects to rise
From the prison of skeletons,
Singing and silkwinged.

Pica

Pica: A craving for unnatural food, as seen in hysteria and
pregnancy.

—*Webster's New World Dictionary*

Child, when I dig through
Fireplaces, gathering in a silver box
Only the whitest ashes, I am thinking
Of you growing fair as a snow queen
Haloed by flames. With my throbbing
Belly as compass, divining, swollen
Rod, I find abandoned buildings
Where I dance under the rain
Of peeling plaster. I harvest
Paint, rolling sheets in my mouth
Like dried fruit. Whatever you wear,
You will outshine the most bedecked.
You will walk through the staring crowds
Who struggle against their racing thoughts,
Imagining you naked, glossy as wet canvas.
From the gardens of the rich
Do I take worm-loosened soil.
Your every word will scatter flowers,
Every gesture a flung fruit.
I turn laundry soap into soup.
The air will hang heavy, chandeliered
With the bubbles of your laughter.
O, what joy in nourishing you, my hungry
Stove, dear child craving coals, feathers,
Tree bark. What you demand, loudvoiced

And fullgrown in my dreams, I give.
With each mouthful, we burn away
All trace of your father, his absence
Glaring like our emptied plates.

"Last night, I danced too much.
Will my baby sprout wings?"
"If I stare all day at the squash
Growing in a neighbor's yard,
Will my baby swell, softbrained?"
"Two days ago, I spiraled down
A flight of steps.
So help me, all you white-haired
Saints, will my baby limp,
A hunchbacked spider?"

They write, on soiled paper bags,
Their scribblings dizzying
As crisscrossing ladders.
On the edges, they draw, wistfully,
Chubby infants with three heads,
Broomsticks for legs.
They beg for salves to cool
The volcano of rising nipples.
How to get rid of the treasure maps
Threading latitudes across their thighs?
They ask how they should sleep,
On one's back, belly, or side,
So as not to dream of windtossed ships,
Or of husbands deciding, from now on,
They will wear the skirts of priests.
Anything, they will pay anything
For recipes to make their babies
Speak in Latin, figure logarithms

On bare fingers, shrug off diapers,
Break from crawling into a run.

The old wives gather at night,
Laughing till their bellies
Ache, tumbling hand in hand over
Their mounds of gold. To keep warm,
They throw letters into the fire.
The air above them crackles:
Broken umbrellas of question marks,
Riot of lightning with no rain.
Even the blind storks know better,
Winging out of their way.

Playing Mahjong with My Father's Ghost

*I*t is spring indoors in Wen Chiu's house.
V/e walk in light, slowly, taking in
What she has made with her hands:
A lake only inches wide, a book-length
Sand garden. On the walls, they glow
As if lit from within, her mother's treasures:
All that the sad, silent woman
Could fit into one box marked "To America."

My fingers grow familiar, instantly fond
Of her mother's tiles of bamboo and wood.
There is much laughter over missed opportunities,
Premature victory. But I am taking the game
Too seriously. I ask, how can one count as much
As nine? What did I do to lose my turn? It takes
Years, Wen says gently. They would grow old
At the table, calculating the next move
Of lifetime friend, now enemy. Curious children
Were shooed away as they had to concentrate,
Growing so intimate with each tile's grooves
That they would come to know which was Lucky
Flower or Widowed Crane, all with one brush
Of the finger, as if each face-down tile was
The smiling mouth of a lover.

But Mother is calling me to the other room,
Far, far away from the din of men's laughter.
The staccato of falling tiles. No good, no good.
That game my father loses himself in,

Where he seems to feel most at home.
She swears never to learn it, and so must I.
Here, she gestures with her tiny fingers,
Let me show you the game of empty hands.
As she stirs a whirlpool in the center of my palm,
Calling in frogs, birds, approaching storms
With her clicking tongue, my father's laughter
And muffled exclamations begin to sound
Like reprimands. Another game ends.
Mother makes me feel her pulse.
Father knocks down his tiles so as not to know them.

Sisters

I Daughter One

Daughter one, you moved always, a swan.
I imagine you born steelnecked, sure-eyed.
And when we ran, I was always left behind,
Toes sinking in the hollow of your footprints.
On you, new dresses flared with the sun,
The skirts struck susurrant and smoldering,
Rubbed by the flint of your limbs. Did your
Beauty blind our parents? The fireworks
Of your laughter left them deaf. How else
Could you have slipped through locked doors,
Leaving behind the snake's tangle of your shed
Clothes? You sometimes send letters
From somewhere always raindrenched, telling
Of your muchkissed husband and the twins
You love equally, refusing to remember
Which one is heir, who first gasped for air,
Suckling claim to your heart.

II The Youngest

On me, your skirts bone rattle.
I move, slow or fast, depending
On how I must dodge the play
Of your shadow. Behind closed doors,
Our parents weep, feeling your cheeks
Across the flap of your still sealed letters.
At night, I ponder the open invitation

Of our front door—am I being asked to leave
Or are they waiting for the green, slithering
Tongued toad? I have mastered the art
Of weaving an elaborate pattern
Out of patience. He will come
When he will come. And when we kiss,
Our lips interlocking like the last pieces
Of a puzzle, the house will rock with the boom
Of the cloth-covered mirrors. Tomorrow,
On their hands and knees,
Mother and father will find me
In the splinters, the silver tears
Of glass showing the grimace
Of their daughter who had to
Drown herself again and again
In order to survive a childhood.

The Wave

That night, the roof flew, singing.
Father rose from the dead, glowing
In the bedsheets that Mother
Embroidered with his initials.
The rain fell and fell.
I caught the drops in my mouth.
And I sang, clear as the bell
On Easter morning. Mother waded
In the kitchen, mixing rain
With the dough. We would look
For Father later, she said.
Meanwhile, watch your manners,
And wave from the window.
The neighbors floated by,
And the parish priest paddled
From the back of the life-sized
Crucifix. Could I play outside,
Please? I would bring back
Noah's dove and the latest map
To our underwater city.
I sealed my heart with a cross
And kissed Mother's hand.
How sure I was then
Of the way home. Somewhere,
Bread continues to rise.
Bedsheets snag on a bare branch.
I then did not realize
How drowning in knowing
Takes many, slow-motioned years.

Cape Hatteras

By day, we run toward the waves,
Friendly and house-sized. We watch
The Coast Guard mock a rescue.
We applaud the beaming victim
Who willingly flailed about his arms
And wilted in the embrace of strangers.
Lunch of lobsters. We eat with our hands.
You carry me across the sand
On your back, just like you did
In the swamps. But he was
Much heavier, a soldier,
And you trudged then
Through weed-tangled waters,
Disturbing the snakes.
As the sun sets, we sit apart,
Quiet, sending postcards,
Saying in a paragraph
Oh, how happy we are. At night,
The lighthouse looks
For its other eye. We wake,
Alarmed. Did we imagine
That one of us whimpered?
By our bedside,
The shells we gathered
Knock against each other,
Recalling the waves.

Summer Cottage, Whidbey Island

Because this house was built
With no nails,
The fairy tale can begin.
Even found objects perched
On shelves: river stones
And dropped feathers
Tremble at the thought
Of their own beauty.

Outside, the fat berries
Sway, making obscene gestures.
Flaunting tossed skirts,
The flowers send the too heavy
Bees lurching home.

As my lover's footsteps near,
The stained glass windows shake,
Sending rainbows caterwauling
Across the knotted floors. Later,
I still smell him in the tea we sip,
Sweetened with the rubble
Of the bee's combs.

He says good-bye leaving me
With a swoon of kisses
And the hot promise
Of a spectacular comeback.
I shiver imagining the unspoken
"When" and "How."

At night it is easy to see
Stars tearing themselves
From the flesh of sky
As my own jewelled wishes.
The moon whipping itself
With branches is a happy gong
I keep in time with: "Happily,
Forever and ever," we hum,
As I sweep crumbs
And fallen hair.

I sleep soundly in my cocoon
Of darkness while outdoors,
My traps gleam, waiting
For the slowfooted bear
Bearing the unfinished
Epilogue.

Anniversary

Someone's at the door with a basket
Of babies. Too late, you run down
To the slap of floodwaters.
Jump the stair by twos. Show him
There's life still in swollen ankles.
He should not have seen you
In your wedding dress too soon.
The pew of old women in church
Warned you. *"Kutob, kutob,"*
Your heart thuds like a stone.
You could not wait, making him
Stand back, as you posed by shelled
Windows, waiting for the church
Bells, stroke of sun, to touch
At perfect angles, the sequined
Roses running over the very rim
Of your breasts. Veiled,
You childishly believed the setting
Sun could turn you virginal.
Sometimes, on damp days, the ring
Gets too tight. You almost chop
It off along with the blue veins
Of his Sunday meat. It's always
At night when he's fast asleep
When the knocking gets worse,
Desperate. *"Kutob, kutob."*
She won't give up, in her rain-
Drenched gown, bearing her
Gifts: spent candles,
Withering baby's breath.

Bride of Okura

Brideless towns are common along ura-Nihon, Japan's back coast, and some seem resigned to atrophy. But the village of Okura has faced the issue head on. A few years ago it sent a local contingent to the Philippines to recruit wives for some of the scores of young farmers without spouses.

—Patrick Smith, *Inner Japan*

Sometimes, I still wake up to Sunday.
I think I hear Father Guido's
Church bells pealing,
Shaking me out of sleep
Into a freshly washed dress
And between the kneeworn pews.
But it is this gong ringing
A paper screen away
Taking lifetimes between tolls.
My mother-in-law warms herself
With a single syllabled chant,
Rubbing her beads interspersed
With coins and tiger's claws.
I hurriedly say my own prayers
And rise to steep the green leaves,
Failing to read in them
The calligraphy of my future.

I am luckier. Erlinda, down the street,
Moans away, balling herself up
In mounds of hay. No one has seen
Natividad for months. Her husband's

Mouth remains shut as their stable door.
Because our son kicks more and more,
Fighting to split my belly,
My husband takes me to the fish house
Where, beaming, he will let me order
Roe, tuna, and sea urchin in halting
Japanese. The cook, laughing,
Brings the fish, still jumping,
Looking for its missing pieces.

At night, when his mother finally
Softens from stone into sleep,
He will ask me, almost shyly,
To name his parts as I bring
Them to life. I speak more fluently
In the dark, my tongue swimming madly,
Fighting against the current.

Someday, he promises to bring me
To the sacred mountains of Dewa,
Where blind women converse with the dead
And where naked men meditate
While immersed in freezing waters.
As the cold enters the house
In the shape of his family ghosts,
I coax myself to sleep. In my mind,
I am making my own trek, a pilgrim
Surefooted in the snow, seeing,
With closed eyes, in all this whiteness:

My son laughing as he calls out
The names of tufted birds, orchids
And thick-waisted trees in the language
I have taught him as he leads me,
Running, all the way home.

Rice and Fish Sonnet

With bare hands we eat in a lamplit room
Rice pearls, steamed fish, honeyed flowers.
Music of the moon strums branches' loom
As wine and wordless talk dissolve the hours.

Tomorrow, we return to fork and spoon,
Clearing away the sad heap of bones
Growing deaf with the dishwasher's dull tune
Growing blind, blinking against the sun's chewed stone.

My love, I grew up to the firescent of spices
In a house bread-dusted, ringing with birds' cries.
You were fatted, alone, with sugar's many guises
And prewrapped meals promising lukewarm surprise.

But for now, let us indulge in love's slow, smoking feast
Becoming one-tongued, joylulled, crowned beasts.

Dreaming Magellan

I am killing him again.
Slow motion he falls
On the shore, his eyes
Growing large as the islands
He dreamed of. His men
Tottering on the wooden
Whales stab their breasts
With frenzied
Fingers. They try
To blind me with
The sun bouncing
Off their turreted hats
But I do not squint.
The eagle gave me eyes.
He begs for water, his god.
I let his soul flow
Toward the edge
Of the world.

My Life in the News

We eat best with our hands.
Chewing fish eyes,
Picking our teeth with the baby bones
Of a half egg, half duck.
In the absence of delicacies,
We swallow snow and our own hot air.
We get full, humming our sweetest songs
Syrupy with moonlight and sadness.
How happy we look always,
Showing off the caves of our mouths.

And how we dance! Fishlike, serpentine,
Birdsure between the bamboo poles,
Balancing crowns of candle fire
Upon our heads. Watch us leap!
Creep through barbed wire, dodging bullets.
We have a gift for turning into smaller things.
The guards at the bases thought they were
Shooting down pigs.

Years under the yoke have made our necks
Pliant. We nod like windblessed flowers.
Flowers scattered the world over, from
Singapore to Paris, watching
Over powdered babies, or being watched
Through beer and cigarette breezes
As we open and close, open and close,
Generous as gods with our secrets.

We are *"brownfaced, under five feet,*
Blackhaired, browneyed." Harmless
When kept at a distance, remote
As our scattered islands. But
Never stop watching us. When
We can shrink no more, we vanish.
Finding no tracks, you grow alarmed
For who now will tell you what to do
In the face of your shadow's disappearance?

The Man Who Cleaned Her Shoes

Each shoe fits snugly into my cupped hands,
A sculpture strangely warm to the touch,
A drinking vessel, a waiting nest.
Hummingbird-beaked heels, oystersoft
Inner linings. The leather tongues
Tap the names of the cold lands
They came from. They murmur
Of where they've been,
Rocking on yachts, sneezing
Through the savannah of carpets,
Or clicking in sympathy on rickety
Boards as she surveyed under
Her parasol the latest disaster:
Her collapsing cultural center,
Or another nameless barrio
Flattened by the floods.
It is said she had 3,000, perhaps
5,000, shoes. How many bullets
Laid end to end will it take
To wrap around the world?
Will there ever be enough rice grains
In the blackened pot? Surely,
More than my widowed mother's tears.
They seem to multiply, as they dance,
Disembodied, on spotlighted
Shelves. But I know each of them
By touch, blindfolded. Here,
A loosened sequin, there, the nearly
Invisible grin of a zipper

For hiding secret papers.
I wipe and wipe till I see mirrors.
For the best I reserve my spit.
By the time I end, I must begin.
I hum as I work, with stained hands.
Above me, snakes rustle.
Laughter muffles a resounding defeat.
As the shoes
Begin to grow cold in my hands
Like orphans, like the best
But rotting cuts of meat,
She will leave
As she first arrived:
Desperately wiping the mud
Of her past
Off her bare feet.

Broken English

for Manuel Fragante, dismissed from his government post
because of his "heavy Filipino accent"

The asuwang has a long, black tongue.
She pokes it through holes in the roof
Rooting for newborn babies. Maria Clara
Totters between the convent spires
Singing in Spanish the lullaby her father,
The friar, taught her. The village
Idiot running naked in the rain chants
The first, middle, and last names
Of all the American presidents backwards.
They are all my mothers. At night,
When the cold burrows in my bones,
They come with bowls of porridge
And unpolished pearls to lay
Upon my burning tongue. Who is my father,
They croon. I murmur in polysyllables:
"Magellan, Hirohito, Macarthur, Ferdinand."
It is when they crowd around me,
Rubbing my blue toes and the hollow
Behind my ears, that I do wonders.
Their eyes drop gems of pride.
Mesmerized, they fold their hands
Into sparrows as their son recites epics,
Proverbs, curses, cryptic cures:
Words darting like the long, flaming
Tails of extinct birds. The rented room
Quivers. I wake, seismic with joy.

O winter of my speechlessness,
The barely there sun is my open mouth.
My tracks leading nowhere celebrate
My silence. I write myself into the sullen snow,
Heavy booted, with glove imprisoned hands.

A Sestina Written in a Cold Land, or There Is No Word for Snow in My Language

I come from a land of saints.
We kept jars of their tears and bones.
Rooms filled with the scents of their wounds.
Warned and warmed by the holiest books,
We remember how martyrs sweated naked in snow
Or roasted over flames, singing in tongues.

But here, I wake, with a slithering snake's tongue.
Please save me, my mother's candle-honored saints!
False promises spill like steaming guts upon the snow.
My venom makes acid of my blood, chalk from bones.
I wilt like a pile of trodden leaves, molding books.
My words fester, yellow as losers' wounds.

Prettiest phrases axe the air, leaving sapping wounds.
I always slip away, barebacked, on the fish of my tongue.
How I lie, blankfaced as the pages of a dull book.
Swearing on my father's grave, invoking a virgin saint,
I rattle hollow as my ancestors' dried bones,
Echoing back the silent stretches of snow.

O, angels, drag wings upon the unbroken snow
That I may wash in your tracks my wounds.
Let me hear my mother sing through my bones
And taste my father's wisdom on my tongue.
I dream of them, hovering over me, sadfaced saints,
Arms wide open as a windswept book.

If I set to flame my borrowed books,
Perhaps I can loosen the grip of snow.
How the fire will halo me, a repentant saint.
The smoke of strange words will clear my wounds.
The ashes of a puppet's accent falls from my tongue.
O, to feel the rush of childhood rhymes in my bones!

But, I have gotten too used to softer bones
And the absence of muchthumbed books.
I wear quite well my secondhand tongue
And can now even walk upright on snow.
Newfound friends, charmed by my wounds,
Tell me I smile just like a carved saint.

It is easy to break a child's bones, smash saints,
Tear final chapters from books, grow flowers from wounds.
But how to sweeten a stale tongue, how to find maps in snow?

Luzviminda, or Filipinas Make Such Good Maids

Migrations that must needs void memory
—Hart Crane

They call me Lucy who call me
From the steamy kitchen to show
Their guests how I can, harmonica-
Like, whistle "Blue Moon" through
A folded leaf. The husband touches
My breasts with his eyes. My womb
Teems islands disappearing at high
Tide. Between my legs lie virgin
Forests where snakes still roam
Upright. His wife shows me how
To turn carrot curls into flowered
Appetizers. I teach her how to grow
Trees indoors. She makes dried-up
Balls out of the scented flowers
No bigger than her bitten nails.
When they cannot sleep, I scratch
The twins' backs simultaneously,
Lulling them with tales of women
Who fly from the waist up above
Church steeples. Their torsos
Tremble under loose skirts, tapping
Thin slippers that peer beneath thorn
Bushes. Tomorrow, they will laugh,
Building a snowwoman whose coals
Are my eyes. Each snowflake I catch
Burns my tongue, burns away the words

To the prayer for warding off
The evil eye's blueness.
In vain, I try to make angels in the melting
Snow but my wingless guardian waits
Where I left her at the customs,
Clutching a passport long expired.
What again is my real name? It rides
And vanishes with my short-lived
Breath. Even the dirty dwarf has given
Up on eating what's left of a heart, mess
Of pale ashes. My thinning shadow
Crosses the snow bridge of burning
Coals, walking on bare feet home.

The Resident Alien as Acrobat

Seen upside down, my smile's a frown.
How polite I am even as my heart pounds
A wolfpaced beat. When I turn around,
I unclench my fist, releasing arrows
Of curses, silently. I walk in a crouch
Disguising kings in my blood and the wings
Fluttering beneath my thin coat.

I have learnt to say "love"
Without wincing, hearing myself
Tossing cheap syllables
Clanging against fancied objects.
No longer will I stop to save
Each snowflake, a miracle
Melting into tears in my cupped hand.
When my throat rages dry,
I recall the dozen ways to say "rain."
Now and then, I let my tongue swim
Against the tide of names: my brothers
And sisters leaping wordlessly
Out of my sight, our likenesses
Blurring into a muted darkness.

But, I survive, you see. Even thrive
Here in this jungle of damp noises.
I bare my teeth, twist my jaws
Like a well-trained chimp. Watch me
Blow cartoon bubbles, form frothy
Lace at the corners of my mouth.

Pardon that strange cry I make.
It is just our way of saying
Both "joy" and "pain."

A Barren Woman Puts on Her Man Costume

Let me tell myself:
It is not out of spite
Especially designed for me
But out of pride in our history
That the village, always,
Must celebrate crucial dates
On nights of the full moon.
I put on my Man Costume.
Loose black shirt, looser
Trousers. That is all.
No need for thickened brows,
Added inches here and there,
Bush above my lips. No matter.
All know who I am.
After the solemn chants
And drumbeats, I know my cue.
The white chickens lying
Catatonic on the ground
Lose their heads to the silver
Axe. I scream and laughter begins.
Steaming rice and palm wine.
Clapping beat trying to keep up
With the frenzy of my feet
Churning dry dust. More laughter.
The girls-grown-to-women
Glance bold-eyed beneath their veils
At the boys-turned-to-men.
Little children, coaxed by the elders,
First throw chicken bones, then larger

Stones. A bruise here, a cut there.
Not enough blood drawn to hurt.
I am driven to the edge
Of the firelit circle.
Now, it is their turn to dance.
First, barely touching, merely mocking
Intimacy. With the heartbeat freed,
They play the ritual of newfangled lust.
All join in, and there, flickering
Near the center, my former husband's limbs
Tangle with the blooming branches
Of my younger sister.
Here, in my exile's hut,
I still feel the throb of drums,
The echo of my womb.
By my feet, ash heap
Of my tossed-off clothes.
This night's torment
Has just taken root.
The moon plants herself
By my window, showing off
Her beautiful emptiness.

The Weeping Fig

> I never read the story of the barren fig tree without trembling.
> —Simone Weil

A forest indoors. Nest of unbroken
Insect kingdoms, invisible hierarchies.
I caress your braided trunk. You shiver,
Intoxicating me with the little gasps
Of your too green leaves. At night,
A rustling. I imagine fruit dropping,
Heavy as moneybags. Petulant lips
Uncurling, hungrily. A bejewelled
Snake climbs up our quivering.
My skirts uncoil upon the floor.
Morning. The too vivid stained
Glass of day. Where to hide
This withering, the scorched
Candelabra of bare bones?
Curse of leviathan proportions.
We are doomed to harbor lust,
Gild the blasted edifice
Of barrenness. We cast
Cold spells, blast all that is
Softshelled with unforgiving harmattans.

Lost Ring

An orphan has found it
In the wreckage of fishbones.

Let her taste in its hardness
Her mother's warmth in homemade bread.

The angry lover kicking stones
Will raise it to the oily lamps

Weeping and laughing, disbelieving
The too late arrival of luck.

Let him see through its many faces
How love, though unreturned, knifes

Through rock. O, my own dear love,
I think of my loss turning to gifts

For strangers with wild hair
And stricken faces. Let the absence

Circling my finger like hellfire
Strike flame, rain blessings

Upon those who will grasp it
As they would a magic stone

That makes one or one's problems
Invisible. In moments like this,

Paring globes of fruit
Or pruning the dead roses,

When the ache travels from finger
Bone to heart, sure as lightning,

Do I imagine other lives made better
By grief. In remembering,

Your smile will candle a distant room.
Bring food to a table, lead the lost home.

Our Island

for the displaced residents of Calauit Island, Palawan

All my years as a fisherman
I've seen strange things,
Like fish with wings and mermaids
Waving from half-submerged rocks,
But the worst shock was seeing
My childhood home forever from a distance.
We were ordered off our island
To make a playground for the president's son.

He had gone somewhere in Africa
On a tourist packaged safari.
Ever since, his hands grew itchy
Unless he caressed his guns.
His eyes twitched, imagining
Houseflies as humped beasts.

He sent his tin soldiers
All across the archipelago
In search of a suitable kingdom
For his lodge made of legos,
Where he could wear camouflage fatigues,
While his beauty queens shed leopard skins.

They found us and called it paradise.
We thought so too and welcomed them
Serving warm beer and leafwrapped rice.
They slept in our homes and left us

With empty bottles and emptier lies.
When they returned, they brandished knives.

At night, we sometimes hear
The stuttering of machine guns.
If we turn ourselves to shadows,
We can paddle close enough
To smell their cooking fires.
Taste giraffe meat and wildebeest's tongue.

In the last election,
The waves swallowed our ballots.
Where we plant seeds, we harvest sticks.
Turtle shells and fishbones don't mix.
My grandfather dreams of new teeth.
Above my newborn's grave, a driftwood crucifix.
We were ordered off our island
To make a playground for the president's son.

The Dangers of This Craft

For your own good, do not claim to be a poet.
—advice of a well-meaning friend

*H*ow we sing, even as we are boiled alive.
Those who torment us strain to sustain
Our last notes. In a landscape
Of sameness, our crooked towers scrape
Sensibilities, the well-trained eye.
Why, when starved, do we thrive?
Remembrance of childhood's bread
Rising. The taste of dulcified
Droppings of air. Our well-
Meaning friends beg us, please,
Speak in the measured tones
Of the mediocre. Show off
Our mastery of muteness,
The ambidextrous virtuosity
Of work-stained hands. Let
Those knitting needles, heavy-
Handled axes fly. Why must
We hear voices? See the moving
Parts of still objects? And so,
We insist we no longer see
Through whitewashed walls.
We confess our dreams of flying
Have ceased. We scheme,
The miracle of money keeping us
Awake. Our pleasure lies
In memorizing the exactness

Of recipes. We are found to be
Most eloquent when quiet, even
As we argue happily with the teeming
Inhabitants opening doors in our heads.
We stare seemingly unmoved at the fire
Of our burning books, all the while
Enthralled, reading secrets in the flames.
They think they've killed us off
Even as somewhere, everywhere, a child
Recalls the beat of the ocean womb.
They dance upon our tombs, unaware
Of how they have fallen
Victim to the rhythm
Of our singing bones.

Things to Do in the Dark

Soon after signing the Electric Power Crisis Act, President Fidel Ramos appealed to the Filipino public for patience and a little sacrifice to help the nation "through a rough road ahead."

—*Philippine News,* April 1993

The poor have nothing else to do
But grope for each other, their solace
Turning into remorse. More and more
Marionette children roam the streets,
Knocking on tinted windows.
The futile wish: Let there be light
To start the coughing of machines.
Bring life to the uniformed
Workers quick with rivets and needles.
"Made in the Philippines" once screamed
The labels of winter clothes
And plastic furniture. But silenced
Now, draped ghosts of steel
Grow crowns of rust as the unemployed
Pound nails, fasten buttons
In their sleep. Inside mansions,
Camouflaged by barbed wire
And bougainvillea, generators imitate
Dragons. Their fumes turn the night sky
Bluish, dragging bedridden clouds
Toward the grave. In air-conditioned
Bliss, the rosy children of the rich
Toss in drifts of scented powder.

Sweat laurels the brows
Of their fathers dreaming
Of chandeliers and exit visas.

When They Left Subic Bay

From out of the undulating smoke, a one-eyed
Prostitute culls configurations of the next war.
The Marine's wife wipes her eyes, but not
Out of nostalgia for the fog-drenched view.
She curses these islands, lost privileges,
Her allergies. Protectively, she clutches
Under her arm a poodle and yesterday's
Stars and Stripes. Outside electrified gates,
Penitents crucify themselves. Overhead,
The final hawk sweep of shadows. Who woke
The potbellied deity under the volcano? His drool
Marches stately through bulletproof bungalows.

Intuition

Shortly before an earthquake, animals, in unison, have been
seen to act in a frenzy, as if frantically trying to escape an invis-
ible enemy.

—*Wall Street Journal*

*T*he clams know. On the ocean bed
They clamber over each other
Forming spindly towers, waiting
For steaming breath to rise
From the earth's crooked grin.
In a neighboring farm,
The bees have disappeared.
Flowers lose their heads;
Their scent offends, rising
To a screech. Against the fence,
A white horse rams itself, again
And again, desperately throwing off
Its unseen rider. Pearl divers
Off southern Japan hear drums
Underwater. By the Amazon,
Alligators raise a cry,
Hundreds of them.
They thrash their tails,
Writing final messages
Upon the swirl of mud.

All is quiet in my white kitchen.
The fluted edges of blown
Glass tremble very delicately.

I wipe the knives, burying
Each in slotted wood.
The front door opens.
There is no rehearsal for this:
The slow dance steps
Toward total devastation.

Survivors will not
Speak of curling up
In coffin spaces,
Drinking their own blood,
Frisking the dead in the dark.
Silence and the horror
Of dreamlessness keep them alive.
In my kitchen, nothing breaks.
The door sings easily on its hinges.
But what I know does not save me.

Gift of Calamities

Ignore the coffins floating by.
What are they to you anyway, the upright
Dead mouthing incoherences, last year's
Seeds rattling in their throats?
Houses cartwheel in mud, rushing toward
The grinning sea. Inday,
Polishing the chandelier's shell lips,
Totters on a stepladder.
Her mother, smoke-colored, gestures
From the cut crystal bulbs. If all
The orphans joined hands, they would encircle
All 7,000 islands. To smother the stench,
Use lime and rubber gloves.
Priests mumble over unmarked mounds.
Guilt lifts, volcanic ash birthing
Blood of sunsets. Omit flowers, please.
Shelter may be found in the guise
Of your anonymous gifts.

Intensity Six: A Call to Dance

Ah love, what a landscape we had.
Each day stagestruck, of sunset and palms.
Suddenly, full tilt, the sun swung.
How easily our house wrenched itself
Mistaking tremors for a call
To dance. Never mind, have we not
Always loved the hammock of darkness,
This locking of limbs now further
Sealed in concrete? Let me kiss
The dust off your brow. I drink
Your slow-trickling wine. From out
Of the corner of my mouth, I'll sing.
How you will laugh at my imitation
Of bulldozers. Evernearing,
They threaten to unearth us. Gently,
Gently, an unseen hand rocks our cradle
Of rubble. We lullaby out of stillness
The once frantic kicks waking your womb.

The Arsonists

Rain of pocketknives.
Unharmed, we flint lightning
From our flesh, joyous . . .
Enjoined. As the clouds
Roll themselves into
Winding sheets,
The old-growth
Pines retreat, threatened
By the heat of our rising
Bodies melting the clock's
Hands backwards, twisting
Doorknobs. A longtailed
Dragon crawls on our roof
Begging to trade his years
For our luck. Innocence keeps
Us supple, knowledge of near
Death triggers that flicker,
Tunnel's end in our eyes.
Let the waters rise
Knocking down road signs.
The dragon sheds his golden
Scales. Bounty of firsts.
We harvest fire.

Empty Room

The last tenant's left
A set of knives. In the absence
Of mirrors, we reflect
Distortions. We clap,
And the ceiling billows
Into a tent. Higher, higher,
The pale magician cries,
And the maiden dreams down
Feathers rising into thin air.
An elephant genuflects,
Commanded by the nightly
Queen's thighs. While we wait
For the movers to arrive,
We keep warm by gypsies
Splintering furniture
For the fire.

China Patterns

My dear, all brides have them.
Hoard of moon faces, gleaming,
Tilted to reflect the captured
Sun. Ritual of polish. Hum
As you wish away shadows, wipe
Hands off the brittle clocks.
Give each piece a secret name,
A child that will cling—miracle
Of gravity—or fall, wheeling
Avalanche, at your call. All
Accidents are foreseen. Your
Future years are gleaned
In the way the handpainted leaves
Or spiked fruit cascade round
And round: ennui's cornucopia.
Mine bore a field of lilies,
Funereal and yellow-tongued.
Alone, as the candles hissed
Their last breath, and the moon
Broke itself into perfect halves,
I hurled my plates toward
The sky, and they lodged there,
With the splintered
Spinster stars. Choose
Your china carefully.
They must fit perfectly
Between his fingers, he
Who gives life to you all.
Recall how you would not

Cry out, child that you were,
When your favorite toys
Fell into pieces falling
Into the hands of pasty
Boys. Choose a pattern
That continues the cycle of
Blossoms even as they break
In his hands. Choose
A pattern you can stand
To lose. And remember,
Refuse to flinch
Even as the pieces
Fly. My dear,
The pattern starts again.
It tries to grow
Between the thorns
Trellising your heart.

Paper Year

Let us celebrate with our household gods.
Call in the family ghosts who have never left.
They glue hurled vases, hum ancient tunes
To muffle our shouts. Tonight, let us
Use our wedding gifts, all silver and outsized.
We dance, fencing with our elbows, boasting
Of how our feet never leave the ground.
We toast to the absence of friends, severed
By our shared disdain. Who could have
Ever liked us? Smoke rises, ashes
Shifting into flowershapes. The very
Ghosts shiver in our glacial drift.
We try to keep warm, throwing
Into the fire the volumes read
Between our spoken lines and the blueprints
For bridges we built, separately,
As we talked in our sleep.

Aubade in Absence

A phantom pain spreads.
I arch my body instinctively,
Throttling air,
Mist giftwraps the trees.
If I wear my palest sweater,
We may collide in fog.
In this season of tangled fruit,
I wait, animal-quick,
Baring blood kisses.
Under my hands,
Your bones will fall
In and out of place.
I follow the spoor
Of your breath.
Better than a widow
Keeping faith,
Or nightly fires,
I set this song
Hours earlier.
My humming grows
Roses for our breakfast
Table, red as my wounds
Keeping fresh.

Shot Through

I have purposely lost the camera.
It is for moments like this,
When the urge hits
To frame you as you are,
The rare sun coasting behind you,
Forest fire of your hair,
Eyes gold as Spanish coins
Reminting themselves in the hull
Of a sunken galleon, that I relish
How beauty's fleetingness leaves
Souvenirs, rose wounds that close
And open, fluttering curtains.
Move quickly out of my mind's sight.
Let me see if I can recast you
Bodied in absence. The blind can
Cartograph a stranger's face
Reading in ridges a childhood
Spent in bed nursing an invisible
Illness or the tossed sheets
Of a more recent unhappiness.
In the lovers' pool in Batangas
I panicked, kicking the warm soda
Waters, ridiculously thinking
The curling fingers of weeds
Were snakes. Just as old couples
Resuscitate their wedding pictures,
I invoke that memory of you laughing
As you saved me from my improvised
Drowning. Click. Another and

Another moment swims in the dark
Room. A tripod hobbles, overpowered
By the weight of joy closing in
As you loom, larger and larger,
Squeezing out the backdrop,
Shadows, time. I walk, slowly,
Deliciously, through your solo
Exhibit, touching you repeatedly,
The fixed stars stabbing my eyes.

Crossing Dreams

> Last night, I, too, wandered lost in the darkness of a disturbed heart.
>
> —Ariwara no Narihira, *The Tales of Ise*

*N*ight of spilled light. You walk
Between the torched trees bearing
A gift nestled in silk. Your hair
Swishing past your robe sweeps up
Broken leaves. Where are your hands?
If I lift up your skirt, I know
I will find your stockinged feet
Dangling inches from the ground,
The blinding sign that your pallor
Does not come from crushed pearls.
I fight the urge to snatch you back,
To make you call out the secret names
We sewed into the inner folds of each
Other's sleeves and grass pillows,
To lock fingers in the gesture
Of promise. Instead, I reach out
For the swirling folds of darkness.
Have you brought what we both wished for
Each other, secretly? Tongue of temple
Bell. Silver dagger. Long-handled
Mirror. With closed eyes, we sense
Each other's peace and move gracefully,
Surrendering to the slow certainty
Of ritual. At last, needing no words,

Smoke slips through lips half pursed.
And how we laugh, seeing in the glass
Only what lies behind us:
The shaven moon, the trees' bare hands.

Good Neighbors

A city night. Quivering fit
Of stillness. Through the film
Of half-sleep, animal cries.
A woman in white, like a blindly
Shot arrow, neon glow, runs
Going nowhere. *Please, oh god,*
Please. Pounding on doors,
Shaking the flowered curtains,
She scrawls her nail-
Driven last words.
They wake to peaceful streets,
Glistening, packed snow. No flurry
Of footprints, no struggle.
They tell the police she was quiet.
Knew no one. She had lived
Among them for six years, walked
Her dog, waved sometimes, cut
Spring flowers wearing gloves.
They cannot recall her name.
But she visits them in dream,
Touching their cheeks, hair,
Fingertips. She draws close,
Her breath stroking their faces.
Her white slip reddens under
The night lamp's glow.
They wake to tears, cries
Of delight. Their babies play
With choice roses found
Growing between shut curtains.

Leaving Doors Unlocked

Night noises. Once, in my aloneness,
It was fear that rattled the door.
A prowler's shadow flamed upon
The ceiling, settling down familiarly
Upon my bed's planked side. Or was it
Only the floorboard's heaving, weary
Of my scentless spoor, one-way exits?
Now, I wake, cat-slow, seeing in the dark
The will-o'-the-wisp of your breathing.
You sometimes laugh in your sleep.
How nights rim with possibilities.
You wake to my burglar fingers.
The neighborhood stirs to showers
Of missing keys, broken chords
Of tripped alarms. Tomorrow,
The city's most wanted thief
Turns himself in. You come home,
Grinning. We dine on juices
Stolen from bone.

Feeling Amazonian

What a night. Stars
In barbed wire. We hug
Intimate as chance
Partners trying to out-
Last all dancers.
Wine sipped between
Silences cloys lips.
How we once kissed.
Hot wax of your kingly
Seals, my tattoo
Of ferret's teeth.
Listen, our song's
Just joined the oldies.
The moon's a pity
Trying to hide
Nine months in clouds.
Once more, for lost
Memory's sake. Pretend
That I'm your Amazon,
And the lock
Of your arms,
Too small a cage.

The Gift Bearer

> You might have fears and worries about joining the Imperial
> Household. But I will protect you for my entire life.
>> —Crown Prince Naruhito to Masako Owada on
>> the day of their engagement

Look at her, standing on the edge
Of the street, smiling toward
The flashing lights, the brash questions.
Who knows what has gone down her throat?
Foreign wine and words, the stroking fingers
Of strangers. True, he loves her
And has said so in his New Year's poetry
Mentioning a hundred cranes when subtlety
Should have reigned in place of unabashed joy.
And now I am sent to her home
Bringing his gifts of rice wine,
Bolts of silk, and a pair of bream.
There is no turning back. She accepts,
With glassy tears for the world to see,
While his eyes proclaim ardency
For a mere commoner. Once, we could not
Even look upon him. His carriage rolled
Past our streets, preceded by sweepers
And soldiers who would neatly slice
Heads off shoulders not bent
At the proper degree. Windows
Shuttered rapidly like wooden
Thunderclaps. His followers threw
Themselves upon the ground, reveling

In his shade. The only women he saw
Floated on paper screens, unsmiling,
Disappearing into the folds
Of their twelve-layered robes.
From a distance, his mother watched
As we taught him the art of brandishing
A paper fan or his ancestor's sword.
And when the time came to choose
His bride, he left the choosing
To us, to our reading of the wild pheasant's
Innards, the warnings scribbled
On deers' antlers. We would know her
More intimately than she knew herself,
From the breadth of her waist,
To her manner of holding a teacup,
Or of laughing silently, behind her hand.
Her pedigree would show in the tying
Pattern of her obi or in the deliberately
Careless strokes of her calligraphy.
And when she finally came to us,
Awe would twist her torso into suppliance,
Her head bowed with the effort
Of hiding her joy. And who would not
Be struck dumb? To spin in her womb
The heir of the sun, to speak to him
All her days, face to face, behind veils,
Whispering in honorifics. Disbelief
Over her good fortune should daze her,
Keep her cowering in his shadow,

Ten paces behind. I hand over his gifts,
Bowing, much too lowly. Let them bask
For now in good wishes and the kiss
Of the open air. Soon, she will cross
The moat, not noticing how the palace walls
Close in, how tradition forces them
On their wedding day to stand apart.
Their wings fold in. We will shape them
As we have for centuries,
Like the paper swans hanging over
His grandfather's grave in stiff garlands.

Farmer Finds Bodies of Student Volunteers

Once in a while, they come up,
Depending upon the unseasonable rains.
Biding time, they find their way
Always to some poor bastard's patch
Gone barren. His son digging for a mayor's
Promise hit them. They lie (was he
Surprised?) in formal rows. Still
In their college spectacles, wearing
Too starched shirts. He remembers
Their grating honorifics, their baby
Hands fumbling with work. He still
Swears he slept through the shots
That night. Never mind, the flowers
Have shot back, the vines strangle
For space. In gratitude, he sends
His son to the Chief of Police's
Palace, bearing their hearts
Almost of sugar, seed-riddled.

Infant Snatched from Stroller at the Mall

*T*hose who love her will not speak of it.
But words like *absence* and *princess,*
Still too dangerously close to being taken
Out of context, continue to prowl
Outdoors. They have, oh, so kindly, drawn
The curtains. After meals, they wait
For her slippered pacing, wondering:
What could she be hoarding upstairs
That is making her invisible load
Only heavier and heavier?

It has been several years now.
She has aged gracefully. Her shelves
Hold feathers, abalone shells, monuments
Of coral. Neighbors speak of her in near
Reverence. They point out her house
As if it were no longer there.
But no one has ever seen
How on moonless nights she flies
Over their small town, staring
Through their open windows,
Eating with her eyes
The laid-out feast
Of sleep-slaughtered children.

The Love of Saints

*W*ho knows who set us on fire?
Torch the path of sickly moons,
Impale fireflies. Here, a scar
From childhood. Your thumb startles
Waters, stirs the crowns of pine.
Axe-wound. Sometimes we get frantic
As vampires, hiding our hunger
By slow seductions. What do we care
If it is merely the moon's tug, atoms
Gone amok, crossed swords? Lightning
Crackles incandescence. We grope for
Light behind closed eyes, remembering
Signposts, the rise of stones.
Shameless, we are only too happy
To grapple before the huddle
Of priests taking notes, counting
Miracles.

From the Bridal Book III

Last night, you talked in your sleep
Muttering our vows. Turn to me,
Child grappling with the worst dream:
A dragon creeping from the cave
Of hoarded failings. I slice onions
To the heart. Through the lacy veil
Of tears, I glimpse the youngest sister
I never had playing in mud
Half naked and happy, sylphic
In my bridal slip. The dried
Bouquet she tosses lands
In the empty fist of a nest.
Oh, soap opera of idle
Afternoons. Let me see
My life from another
Point of view, out
Of breath, hanging
From the cliff's ledge.
My husband, on his way
Home, takes another route,
Slipping out of himself,
Raw-skinned and small
In the distance.

Tonight, it will be your turn
To cuddle the child
Frightened at the rain.
Assault of blessed rice
Upon our roof. Send him away,

The black-robed priest tapping
Our window. Let him walk
My father home, who still waits
For the first waltz
Under the tightlipped moon.

Family Tree

Storm-struck, our tree bristles into
A raving woman, lightning singing
Through its limbs. But it grows
Anyway, every day, every hundred years,
Tiny flower hats and mangled fruit.
Grandfather scooped out of its belly
A fistful of ants, red with fury,
Circling their pearl babies,
The fat, sleeping queen. Grandmother
Wailed the morning after her wedding,
Her hair having gone stark white.
She let it grow past her knees,
Her bridal train following her,
A glistening shadow. Grandfather
Walks with a cane, smartly, as if
He were naked, his limp turning
Into a dance. The churchbound ladies
Hide behind their netted fans.
He was known, past his youth, to have
Climbed the convent walls. Mother
Pins my hair, pulling until she draws
Tears. This way, she says,
Grandfather's stories will pour
Out of your ears. He is smart, you see.
Once I get over my fear of wings,
He promised, I would catch sight
From the summit of the tree
Grandmother as a child, trailed
By a stallion nudging her bare nape

And Father, growing larger and larger
As he leaves behind the black
Crawl of the funeral parade.

Walking with the Dead

Half of a Siamese pair, he now
Walks through the antique shop
Fingering pocket watches, holding
Them close to the thud of his heart.

On her thirty-sixth birthday, she
Will wear under her flimsiest gown,
No slip, and do cartwheels
When the sun looms at its highest.

They walk in step, their shadows running
Ahead, embracing trees. In India,
She screams in love or wrath, crumpling
In the heart of scented fire.

Explaining the Origin of My Name

I

Curiosity, it means. Woman peeking
Through bullet holes, diamond pattern
Of half-shut hands. Woman unknotting
Men's talk, that nurtured sense
Of following history's affairs,
Through the din of kitchen pans.
She sits as if caught in the web
Of her own stitches, so still,
As if she has turned into another
Leg or armrest of the hardbacked
Chair. Her husband, hunting outdoors,
And her children, imagining themselves
Explorers in another land,
Raise hands to mouths, hearing
Themselves respond. She commands,
Silently, through the veil
Of vegetable-brained questions.
They stop in their tracks,
Seeing always, ahead of their own,
Her slippers' shufflings, and the wake
Of her chastising broom.

II

Almost apologetically, I disclaim
All rights of the Prophet's daughter.
And the life with only my eyes
To show, squirming in the cocoon

Of loose black veils. My name
Is "Fa-tima" without the peacock's
Tail of an *h*, with the stress
Falling on the wrong accent,
Too eagerly, like a bare-kneed
Servant girl leaning heavily upon
Half-shut doors. My mother,
Carrying the crucifix
Of her unborn child, climbed the steps
To the other Fatima, a windswept cove
In Portugal, shielding her dripping
Candle as she unlinked bead after
Dark bead, mystery upon mystery,
Of her life's Joys turned to Sorrows
Cycling back to Glories. She knelt
Where the three kerchiefed children,
Behind the armature of fingers
Vainly netting their eyes, witnessed
The burning bush and the sad-faced
Woman under the heavy crown,
Crushing snakes with her bare feet.
And so I was named after a miracle.
And a prophecy. They share a secret:
Lucia, aging nun counting shadows
Falling across grilled windows,
And my mother, disappearing
Into the clouds of dust
Rising from her grandchildren's
Thundering feet. Two women

Wait in Lisbon and in Manila,
Wait for the cleansing fire
Of the beginning and end
Of the world while I fret,
Bruising myself
Against the gentle bonds
Of sacred syllables,
Fighting against the fears
Which have no names.

Kitchen Fires

Oh, we are dangerous, we grinning cooks.
I play with an invisible mustache,
Smack ghostly lips, grow nauseously full
From remembered crumbs. I sway
Brewing a clear soup. In its stirred
Lakes, Mother's distress signals bubble
From hollowed bones. Above,
In chandeliered chambers, my grill-gilded
Sculptures splinter into leftovers.
The guard dogs howl expectantly while
I suck rain from garden stones.
Fever-fast, word winds down marble
Stairs to the laundry yard. Even
The bodyguard asks for my name.
Minutes before his hasty departure,
The Master, through his lace napkin,
Praised my dinner. This wreath
Of rumor is my only reward.
When I brandish the knife, slit
Whatever struggles in my hands,
My eyes glaze over with the stare
Of fish drowning in air. Despair
Of trapped steam. Gem-gleams
Of blood. Oh, how I love setting
Kitchen fires. Waving my apron,
I resuscitate the flames.
I spit on the sizzling ruins.
For my repentance: I fashion

From the melted pots wrist bands
For the Master and Mistress, knots
Of blackened gold to circle their fine bones.

Forsaken Art

*H*er happiness replicates, shaping
Into wall-sized murals of butterfly
Wings crystallizing into human eyes,
Bowstring smiles. In the next town,
A clerk spends half his life splintering
Matchsticks for the brittle castle
Miniaturizing his room. Outside filigreed
Windows, trees raise torn arms,
Dodge the singing bullets.
Women hopscotch over mines.
The dead left on the streets mold
Into sculptures. The artists dream
On, like medieval monks going blind
Leaning over sheepskin and
Scriptures, seeing apocalyptic visions
Through the smoke-dying candles.
Patiently they wait for their muses
To fly, ashes over their heads.
Meanwhile, cities glow, stoked
By civilized fires.

A Rice Grain Village

based on a Beijing artist's rice grain carving

Welcome to our happy village.
Come, sit in the shade, here
By the rock called Viper's Head.
A slice of sweet gourd, perhaps?
The Emperor on his sickbed
Suckled on the rind and instantly
Jumped upon his stallion.
He ate even the seeds as he watched
His enemies' heads pitched upon
His walls. See our lake, calm
As the Jade Princess's looking glass.
There the cranes rattle their brush-
Stroke legs, the cormorants collapse
Their throats. Yes, those are
The beginnings of a dragon's brows,
The lazy ribbons of his breath.
But do not be alarmed,
Since he has just been fed
A pack of thieves
And three sister witches.
Turn to the East. There is no
Counting the farmers, their wives,
Their rock-kneed children
Gathering the harvest. You can
Almost hear them sing for joy.
I sit here and play my flute,
The wind bearing my song

Plaintive as broken plows.
See my Lord's manor.
How lovely the clawed
Roof, how blinding the red-edged
Mirrors fending off the hungry
Spirits. Look at the highest
Window. His fourth mistress
Waves at us, her heavy bangles
Rivaling the sun. She would run
To this hill if she could,
But her feet hold her back
As they shape themselves
Into the closed lips of lilies.
What, leaving so soon?
You must come back
At the onset of winter
When the lightest snow
Turns the graveyard into
A sculptured garden.
The wailing women stir
Even the dragon to tears.
The Tower Lady's zither cracks
The mirrored lake.
I then play my flute best
As sweet gourds harden,
Their empty bellies
Sounding the war call.

Close to drowning, that is happiness.
Each breath knives, keeps us alive.
Meteorlike, rushing through the tunnel's
Mouth, joy chases its own crescendo.
We glorify in conclusions
Always finding the next to the last page,
Undrawn curtains.
Reckless as infants discovering fire,
Wild mushrooms, the lure of heights,
We grow fangs, relearn the rhythm
Of a crawl. The years tumble,
Disarray of lost numbers. We count
Backwards to the day we burned
Maps. No one can rescue us.
We rely on each other's eyes.
Our island drifts farther, evading
Search lights. Angry waves carve
Us into arrows, singing bones. We read
In the dark, unchaining chapters,
Thumbing pages writing themselves
From out of our flesh, shared pulse.

From the Bridal Book II

Months before, the birds came.
The cook and gardener coaxed them
Waving aprons, scattering seeds
Until they filled the eaves
With their tasseled nests.
Now, my mother can sleep.
The house beams warble with good
Fortune. She dreams of eggs
Fissuring, each nestling bringing
More and more luck. Let them
Keep the droppings unswept.
My handsewn gown will drag
The richness off the ground,
Add feathers to my slowing feet.
The children will come as
Many as the sparrows knocking
Nails upon the roof.
Dust flies as they run, flapping
Tender arms. I can hardly see them
Through clouds, cascade of feathers.
Instinct leads them where I cannot
Follow, their hearts beating through
These shuttered windows.

Echo Lake

Running, slanting away from rain,
He imagines lightning traveling through
His veins, the smell of his own burning.
If he survives, perhaps he'll see
Things differently, wrinkles on strangers'
Hands, walking trees, flowerlined graves.
He passes the family of immigrants
Fishing with one line. The grandfather
Shows a toddler how to slice trout
Reverently, gently sliding a heart
Back into the waiting mouth of water.
The mother looks up, without surprise,
As if she has seen him elsewhere,
Radiant, on fire. She stays
Calm. Their fates intertwine even
As she turns away, turns toward
The lake yielding secrets into
Her netted hands. He runs on
Pursued by rain. The family men
First eat the eyes. Lightning rims
The nearby forest where a tree
Sunders itself to find its heart.

Ferry to Bainbridge Island

for Joseph Rosa

We count our wounds in the sun.
Rare blue day and our scars flower.
Old man, you stare at the skyline
Of Seattle and see the old country
With its sparkling tombstones.
Smooth sailing. No rocks to cymbal
The waves. Arrowheads of gulls
Target the silverbacked fish.
All follow precisely instinct's
Invisible lines. A woman
In gauzy black clenches
The handrails. Jump, her father
Calls from the rippling blue grass.
The ship's horn saves her, sexless
Siren promising survival. Remember
The rainbow's end in an abandoned
Car. We ache where our wings once
Were, slide unsteadily on the flatlands.
On the other side, we will breathe easier,
Having conquered the rising tide
Of sickness, relying on sailor's luck.
Perhaps no one will see the black
Coastline of our hearts. Somewhere,
There still must be uninhabited islands.

Upon Losing One's Map

Begin with stillness.
The rhythm of your pulse
Turns you into a compass.
Follow the wish
Of empty hands,
The feet allowed to roam
Unbidden.
Give up your urge
To send signals,
To mark trails,
With memory
Of broken twigs, gathered stones.
You will look back only
Once, to marvel at
The monuments of shadows.
What lies behind you
Has vanished, swallowed
By the wind moving
Boundaries. Ahead
Glints the lure of space.
North, South, East, West
Surrender their fixedness
To the power of your senses.
There is no hurry.
There are only endless gifts
To getting nowhere:
That flash of the familiar,
When what was unknown
Begins to beg for recognition.

The Ohio State University Press / *The Journal* Award in Poetry

David Citino, Poetry Editor

1994	David Young	*Night Thoughts and Henry Vaughan*
1993	Bruce Beasley	*The Creation*
1992	Dionisio D. Martínez	*History as a Second Language*
1991	Teresa Cader	*Guests*
1990	Mary Cross	*Rooms, Which Were People*
1989	Albert Goldbarth	*Popular Culture*
1988	Sue Owen	*The Book of Winter*
1987	Robert Cording	*Life-list*

The George Elliston Poetry Prize

1987	Walter McDonald	*The Flying Dutchman*
1986	David Weiss	*The Fourth Part of the World*
1985	David Bergman	*Cracking the Code*